GET INFORMED—STAY INFORMED

HOUSING AND HOMELESSNESS

Natalie Hyde

CRABTREE
PUBLISHING COMPANY
WWW.CRABTREEBOOKS.COM

Author: Natalie Hyde
Series Research and Development: Reagan Miller
Editor-in-Chief: Lionel Bender
Editors: Janine Deschenes and Ellen Rodger
Proofreaders: Laura Booth, Wendy Scavuzzo
Project coordinator: Melissa Boyce
Design and photo research: Ben White
Cover design: Katherine Berti
Production: Kim Richardson
Print coordinator: Katherine Berti
Consultant: Emily Drew, Public Librarian, B.F.A., M.S.-LIS.

Produced for Crabtree Publishing Company by Bender Richardson White

Photographs and reproductions: Front cover: Shutterstock; Interior: Alamy: 13 (ImageBroker), 17 (Prisma by Dukas Presseagentur), 19B (dbimages), 20C (Enigma), 29 (Bob Daemmrich), 30–31 (Bob Daemmrich), 39T (Jeffrey Isaac Greenberg 19+), 40–41 (Azim Khan Ronnie). Getty Images: 6–7 (Erik McGregor), 8–9 (François Guillot), 19T (Erik McGregor), 24 (Liu Guanguan), 26–27 (Dania Maxwell), 31 (Richard Lautens), 35T (Chloe Collyer/Bloomberg), 37 (Steven Ferdman), 38–39 (Allen J. Schaben/Los Angeles Times). Penguin Random House: 11 (Cover image courtesy of Penguin Random House LLC). Shutterstock: heading band (Josheph Sohm), tablets icon (Oleksiy Mark), key, risk, and graphics tablet images, 1 (Philip Pilosian), 6, 7 top (DC Stock Photography), 10 (Imageportal), 12 (GaudLab), 14–15 (Suzanne Tucker), 15 (Everett Collection), 16 (Volodymyr Kyrylyuk), 20 (MS Photographic), 22 (Monkey Business Images), 23 (Monkey Business Images), 33 (Sundry Photography), 36–37 (Ruben M Ramos), 42–43 (GaudLab), 43 (Oleksiy Mark). Topfoto: 35C (Jim West).
Diagrams: Stefan Chabluk, using the following as sources of data: p7: From national surveys, 2019. p18: U.S. Census 2020. p.21: U.S. Department of Housing and Urban Development/Statista.com. p23: Homeless Hub, Canada. p25: U.S. Census Bureau/Stanford University/statista.com. p28: National Alliance to End Homelessness, U.S.A. p31: Economic Roundtable/L.A. Homeless Services Authority. p34: National Alliance to end Homelessness, U.S.A.

Library and Archives Canada Cataloguing in Publication

Title: Housing and homelessness / Natalie Hyde.
Names: Hyde, Natalie, 1963- author.
Series: Get informed--stay informed.
Description: Series statement: Get informed, stay informed | Includes bibliographical references and index.
Identifiers: Canadiana (print) 20210187700 | Canadiana (ebook) 20210187719 | ISBN 9781427150875 (hardcover) | ISBN 9781427150912 (softcover) | ISBN 9781427150950 (HTML) | ISBN 9781427150998 (EPUB)
Subjects: LCSH: Homelessness—Juvenile literature. | LCSH: Homeless persons—Juvenile literature. | LCSH: Housing—Juvenile literature.
Classification: LCC HV4493 .H93 2022 | DDC j362.5/92—dc23

Library of Congress Cataloging-in-Publication Data

Available at the Library of Congress

Crabtree Publishing Company

www.crabtreebooks.com 1-800-387-7650

In Canada: We acknowledge the financial support of the Government of Canada through the Canada Book Fund for our publishing activities.

Published in Canada
Crabtree Publishing
616 Welland Ave.
St. Catharines, ON
L2M 5V6

Published in the United States
Crabtree Publishing
347 Fifth Ave
Suite 1402-145
New York, NY 10016

Printed in the U.S.A./062021/CG20210401

CONTENTS

1 THE HOUSING SITUATION

A home as a place to sleep, eat, and feel safe is something we often feel is guaranteed. But two percent of the world's population, which is about 150 million people, do not have any housing. Even more than that—about 1.6 billion people, or 20 percent of the world's population—do not have **adequate** housing. Below-standard housing and homelessness are complex problems that do not have simple solutions.

> *"I quickly realized how easy it is for someone to lose housing and how that can eventually lead to losing hope. It was a daily chore to remind myself that homelessness was a temporary situation."*
>
> Ethan Ward, 37, resident of Los Angeles

QUESTIONS TO ASK

Within this book are three types of boxes with questions to guide your critical thinking about housing issues. The icons will help you identify them.

THE CENTRAL ISSUES

Learning about the main points of information.

WHAT'S AT STAKE

Helping you determine how the issue will affect you.

ASK YOUR OWN QUESTIONS

Prompts for gaps in your understanding.

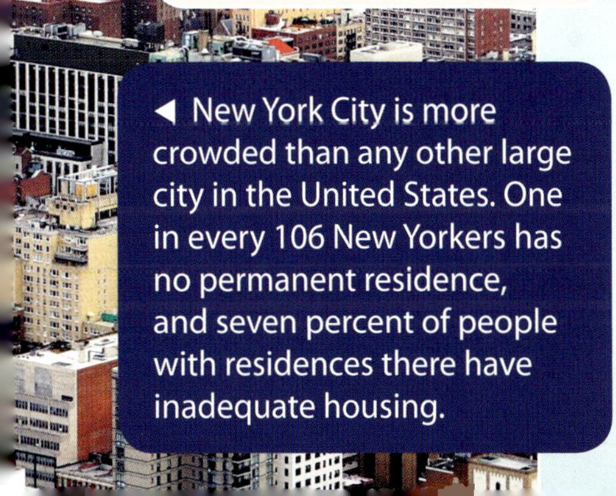

◀ New York City is more crowded than any other large city in the United States. One in every 106 New Yorkers has no permanent residence, and seven percent of people with residences there have inadequate housing.

CAUSES AND EFFECTS

Buying, renting, or building adequate housing is **hindered** by many problems. These include, but are not limited to, rising prices, overcrowding, poorly built structures, terrible landlords, **discrimination**, **systemic racism**, ineffective laws and regulations, and poor funding. From health to security, having no housing, unstable housing, or poor housing affects all parts of people's lives. It also affects community welfare and the national **economy**. Homelessness is a complicated social issue. People become homeless for many reasons including poverty, poor mental and physical health, violence in the home, and lack of affordable housing options.

TAKING THE FIRST STEPS

The **economy**, high unemployment, and lack of support for addiction and mental health issues continue to contribute to the rising rate of homelessness. Recently in the United States, more than 26 million people—about 14 percent of the population—reported that they had experienced homelessness in their lifetime. As individuals, we often think we cannot make a difference to such big problems. Understanding the causes of inequality in housing is the first step to finding solutions. To do this, you need to consider all of the groups affected by the issue. Evaluate their sources of information, listen to their viewpoints, and make decisions.

WHY STAY INFORMED?

DEFINITIONS

Landlords are individuals, groups, or organizations that are the owners of property.
Residents are people living in or on a property, which they may own, share, or lease or hire from a landlord.
Residential refers to anything involving houses and homes.
Unhoused is a term that describes a person who does not have a place to live. It is a less negative and often preferred term for "homeless."
Precariously housed is a term that describes people who face challenges that leave them without a permanent home. It may include people who live temporarily with friends, or those for whom a job loss would mean homelessness.

Homelessness is a temporary situation for some people and an ongoing one for others. Communities, societies, and governments constantly adapt to the changing world, so housing needs continue to vary. To keep up to date with the topic, you must use the most accurate and recent information.

Researchers gather **statistics** and results, looking for problem areas and **vulnerable** groups. Graphs and charts can give you data at a glance. They also help you see how a problem has changed from year to year, or area to area. Researchers also look at other regions and countries to see how they have handled the housing issues. This can give an insight into what methods might work to reduce the number of unhoused and precariously housed individuals in North America.

THE CENTRAL ISSUES

People who are homeless but find temporary housing with friends or relatives are called "concealed homeless." They are less visible to the public. Why is it important to recognize all types of homelessness when thinking about solutions to the problem?

▲ The U.S. Department of Housing and Urban Development (HUD) has created a website called the HUD Exchange (www.hudexchange.info). This is an online platform to gather housing-related news, data, services, and programs in one place.

▼ The COVID-19 pandemic in 2020 resulted in many people being out of work and out of money. This protest in July 2020 in New York City was to demand that city officials suspend rent so people would not lose their homes.

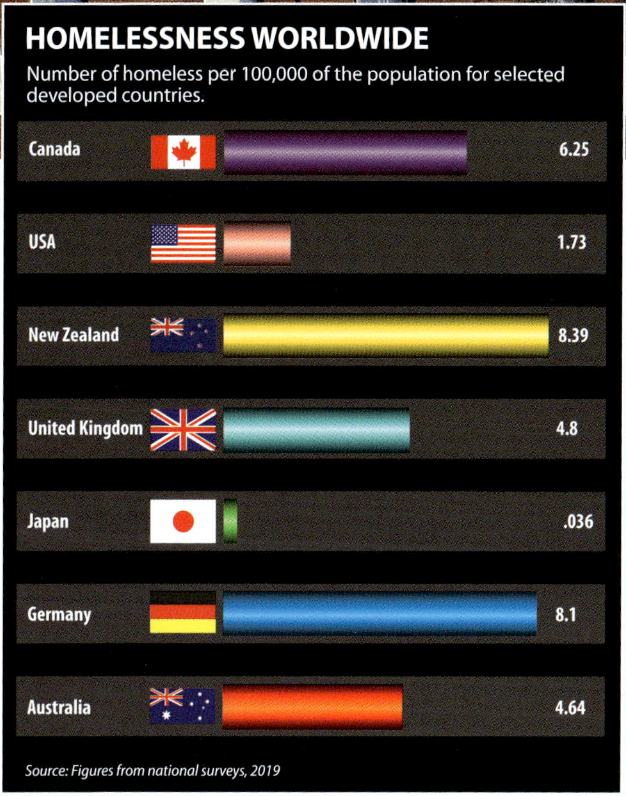

UNDERSTANDING AND LEARNING

The causes and size of the housing problem are constantly changing, so solutions must change, too. Only when you understand all the factors that have an impact on who has difficulty finding or keeping good housing can you add your voice to those who demand new programs or funding to help the situation. This understanding also allows you to grasp the fact that almost anyone's situation can be affected by job loss or poor health, and lead to housing challenges. Knowing how many people experience housing problems creates **empathy** and understanding for people struggling with this issue.

Getting informed on a subject includes learning how the issue developed through history, who has the power to fix or change the problem, and how different groups within the population are affected by it. Staying informed relies on finding accurate material, interpreting information in a logical way, and ways to keep up to date.

2 HOW TO GET INFORMED

Most people have heard of the problem of homelessness. You may have even seen homeless people in your community. But knowing how to approach such a sensitive and complex topic can be difficult. As with every issue, there are different sides and ideas when it comes to dealing with and finding solutions for it.

KEY PLAYERS

Professionals involved in housing and homelessness include:

Social workers help people improve their well-being.

Urban planners help design and regulate the use of land in a city.

Developers buy land, get permits, and prepare land for building construction.

City officials work with city councils to develop programs to promote the interests of citizens.

Government agents are elected to help create or support laws that address the concerns and welfare of their communities.

Mortgage lenders lend money to people or organizations to buy homes or buildings.

Public librarians help people access housing information in libraries.

THE CENTRAL ISSUES

Why does the issue of homelessness create debate and controversy? Why do some people see it as an individual's problem, not a community's problem?

> *Homelessness is not a choice, but rather a journey that many find themselves in.*
>
> Dr. Asa Don Brown, American author, speaker, and clinician

BUILDING UP A BODY OF KNOWLEDGE

Understanding the causes and solutions to the problem means getting to know the key players. Learning about housing and homelessness involves listening to and reading reports from social workers, government and city officials, mental health and addiction counselors, employment agencies, and unhoused or precariously housed people themselves. Each group or individual will provide a piece of the puzzle so that when you put them together, you will get a full picture of the issue.

Next, you must learn key background information and vocabulary. This information often includes timelines. These provide a **visual** or outline of the factors that make an issue begin, worsen, get better, or sometimes end. Looking at a timeline of how the problem of homelessness has evolved can give you clues to the events that affect it and the measures that may solve it. Key vocabulary with this topic includes technical terms that define different types of buildings, and factors that may lead to homelessness. These terms may refer to mental health issues, employment terms, and various types of actions and stakeholder groups.

▲ Tents of **refugees** from North Africa and Afghanistan fill a makeshift camp along the St. Denis Canal in Paris, France, in July 2020. Due to the COVID-19 pandemic, organizations and aid groups that were supposed to help the refugees were shut down to stop the spread of the infectious disease. This meant the refugees remained homeless.

When you begin to get informed about a new topic, you need to find source material. This is any source that gives facts, figures, or other data. Sources can be written, **oral**, or visual. Written source material includes reports, articles, books, newspapers, and text on websites. Oral sources include podcasts or recordings of events, news, or interviews. Visual sources can be charts, graphs, images, documentaries, or photographs.

WHERE TO LOOK

Source material is found in many different places. Libraries are a good place to start your search because they typically have a wide variety of sources, such as books, magazines, and research journals, as well as access to the Internet. Archives are places where there are collections of source materials on a certain topic, group, or time in history. The Internet holds a vast amount of source material, but it comes with challenges.

THE CENTRAL ISSUES

What role would bias play in a land developer's report on how best to use a piece of land? How might it differ from a report by an antipoverty group on the same piece of land?

▼ Newspapers from around the world—filled with primary and secondary source materials—give a range of perspectives on the latest news. Some have a clear political bias; others try for a balanced view.

▲ The girl in this novel lives in a van. Stories like this give readers an insight into homelessness. Researchers believe there are about 2.5 million homeless children in the United States.

KEY INFORMATION

Primary sources are made by people who experienced or witnessed events or situations first-hand. Examples include statements from men, women, and children who are or have been homeless. **Secondary sources** are reports, interpretations, and analyses of primary sources. A magazine article about the effect of homelessness on downtown businesses is a secondary source. **Tertiary sources** are summaries or databases of primary and secondary information. They include entries in encyclopedias.

HISTORY AND BIAS

Anyone can create a website and publish content. It is sometimes difficult to figure out what information is accurate on the site—and what has not been properly researched. Many historians use the Time and Place Rule to help them judge the source material they find. This rule states that the closer in time and place a source and its creator were to an event in the past, the better the source will be.

Even reliable sources may still have a focus or slant to one side of a debate. This slant is called bias. Bias in source material is not necessarily bad, but it is important to be aware of it. Knowing that the data is presented to support a certain view can help you make **objective** conclusions based on your research. Biases around the issue of homelessness and housing can vary. Biases can be for or against government supports for housing. Biases can also influence how people think about homelessness and homeless people.

THE INTERNET AND OTHER MEDIA

Today, most of us turn to the Internet as a place to gather information. But it is important to be informed about Internet research. There are many websites that look impressive, but do not have **credible** information. Sometimes, groups exaggerate the amount of support they have or they post data without the science to back it up. The trouble is, it is often hard to tell if data is valid. People who post opinions as facts, or viewpoints without evidence, can sound very convincing. They break down trust in what you read or see online. This means it's hard to separate accurate from inaccurate news.

One solution is to look for supporting material for anything you read online. Look for scientific studies that back up claims on websites. Search for scientists who specialize in the topic you are researching. Policy experts, planners, think tanks, and charitable foundations are some of the experts to listen to when discussing how to address the lack of affordable housing or the need for shelters.

ASK YOUR OWN QUESTIONS

To determine if a source is credible, consider:

- Does the creator have solid credentials and expertise in the topic?
- Does the headline match the story?
- Is the publisher known to be reliable?
- What sources did the creator use?
- Is the source relevant and up to date?
- Is the source meant to be a joke or **clickbait?**

▼ Websites such as FactsCan, Snopes, and Hoax–Slayer help verify if stories and articles are based on fact or not.

▼ "Gentle density" homes, like these in San Francisco, California, are houses such as semidetached, row homes, townhomes, and multiplexes. Gentle density homes take up less space and cost less than detached homes. They can be ideal family homes in areas of high **population density**.

A VARIETY OF SOURCES

Try to look for source materials in quality newspapers, such as *The Huffington Post, The New York Times, and The Globe and Mail,* and in magazines including *Time* and *Maclean's.* CNN, PBS, and *CTV National News* television have news programs and documentaries on housing. Social media, textbooks, and radio stations can have interviews and personal stories. Governments create and make public reports, graphs, and statistics. Government websites have pages that focus on the economy, unemployment, and on programs for precariously housed people. Scientific journals publish papers on how different regions have tackled problems of homelessness and precarious housing.

3 HOMELESSNESS ISSUES

In North America, housing comes in many shapes and forms. Homes can be detached buildings or attached to other units such as in townhouses, condominiums, and apartment towers. Public housing is housing that is owned by a government authority and rented to people at a lower cost. Social housing is housing owned or managed by government or non-profit organizations with lower rental fees. Adequate housing means a shelter that is a safe, secure place for people to live.

> *"Public housing is more than just a place to live, public housing programs should provide opportunities to residents and their families."*
>
> Carolyn McCarthy, American nurse and politician

KEY PLAYERS

Habitat for Humanity International is a nongovernmental and nonprofit organization. Its mission is to build, renovate, or preserve homes for people who might not otherwise qualify for a mortgage or homeowner's loan. The idea is for people needing housing to work side-by-side with volunteers to build affordable homes at no profit. To date, Habitat has helped more than 29 million people worldwide.

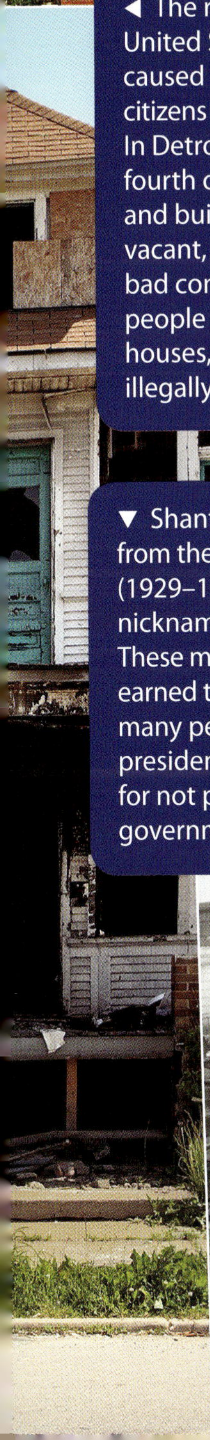

◀ The recession in the United States in 2008 caused nearly 10 million citizens to lose their homes. In Detroit, Michigan, one-fourth of the city's houses and buildings are still vacant, many of them in bad condition. Unhoused people squat in some houses, meaning they illegally live in them.

▼ Shantytowns resulting from the **Great Depression** (1929–1940s) were nicknamed Hoovervilles. These makeshift living areas earned their name because many people blamed then-president Herbert Hoover for not providing more government support.

A HISTORIC PROBLEM

Unhoused people are individuals or families who have no permanent shelter. In North America, experts estimate that almost 600,000 people are homeless on any given night. Some cannot afford housing. This may be because of poverty caused by job loss, injury, illness, or the death of a family member. People fleeing violence in their family also often end up homeless. War, conflicts, **mass immigration**, and natural disasters also contribute to the number of homeless.

In North America, homelessness is not just a modern problem. In the past, governments forced **Indigenous** populations to move from their traditional territories to make room for European settlers. Even today, many Indigenous groups fight for the right to control their lands and secure the funds for housing that was agreed upon in the **treaties** they signed.

The Great Depression was a time of high unemployment. Banks and landlords forced people out of their homes and farms. Those people ended up in temporary camps and **shantytowns**, which existed for more than a decade. Today, new camps have appeared for the poor.

WHAT IS AFFORDABLE HOUSING?

Governments define affordable housing as adequate housing that does not cost more than 30 percent of a family's income. The buildings do not need major repairs, and they have enough bedrooms for the family. A "housing wage" is the hourly sum of money a person who works full-time must earn to pay for affordable housing. In many areas of the U.S., the housing wage for a two-bedroom apartment is about $24. **Minimum wage** in the United States ranges per state from $5.50 to $12.50 for workers who don't receive tips. In Canada, provincial minimum wages range from $11.90 to $15. Most organizations define a "liveable wage" as beginning at $15 an hour.

Affordable housing can be public housing or housing built by non-profit organizations. Builders tend to make more money on larger, detached homes. For this reason, they prefer to build single-homes instead of affordable housing. Over time, neighborhoods change. Less expensive neighborhoods may be gentified, or fixed to suit people who have more money. This drives up housing prices and makes it no longer affordable for lower or middle incomes.

◀ Luxury high-rise apartments, like these in Vancouver, British Columbia, Canada, are priced out of reach of many people. As more are built in city cores, lower-income families and first-time buyers are forced out of these areas.

▲ Inadequate housing and homelessness are widespread problems on tribal reservations in the U.S. and First Nation reserves in Canada. This one in South Dakota has overcrowded housing. It is difficult for people who live on reservations to get bank loans to improve housing. Banks use property as security for repayment for home loans. But banks cannot own property on reservations and reserves, which is held only for tribal and First Nations groups.

DON'T PUT IT HERE

Some people living in detached homes do not want to live near affordable housing complexes. They may believe that **denser**, cheaper housing will lower the value of their property. Yet research done in New York City showed this does not happen. In most cases, neighborhood housing prices remain the same as long as the affordable housing has an attractive design and is well taken care of. In some areas, well-built affordable housing can actually increase nearby property values.

Affordable housing is sometimes difficult to build because of zoning laws, which limit what the land can be used for. Zoning laws might state that land must be used for industry. Many cities are now moving to "inclusionary zoning" instead. This means all new residential development plans must include some affordable housing.

THE CENTRAL ISSUES

If the economy is booming, and the unemployment rate is very low, why is homelessness still a problem? What other factors affect it?

In some places, housing has become so expensive that people can't afford a home even if houses are available. In Vancouver, Canada, and in Seattle, Washington, house prices are rising even though the city populations have been decreasing. This is because the demand for homes is coming not from people living there, but often from housing speculators who buy low and sell high to profit from the market.

City officials and government representatives often do not act to slow or stop rising prices because higher property values generate higher taxes. This often means land gets developed as single-family home subdivisions or industrial and business parks, rather than affordable housing areas.

ACTION ON MANY FRONTS

Some people and **housing advocacy** groups are working to end homelessness. Organizations, such as the National Alliance to End Homelessness in the United States and the Canadian Alliance to End Homelessness, use research and data to find solutions to housing problems. They also work to create resources for unhoused and precariously housed people in the community. Federal, state, and provincial advocacy panels advise and **petition** governments for new laws, funding, and programs to deal with the issue. Other ways they help include:

- locating available affordable housing
- completing housing applications
- obtaining identification for applications

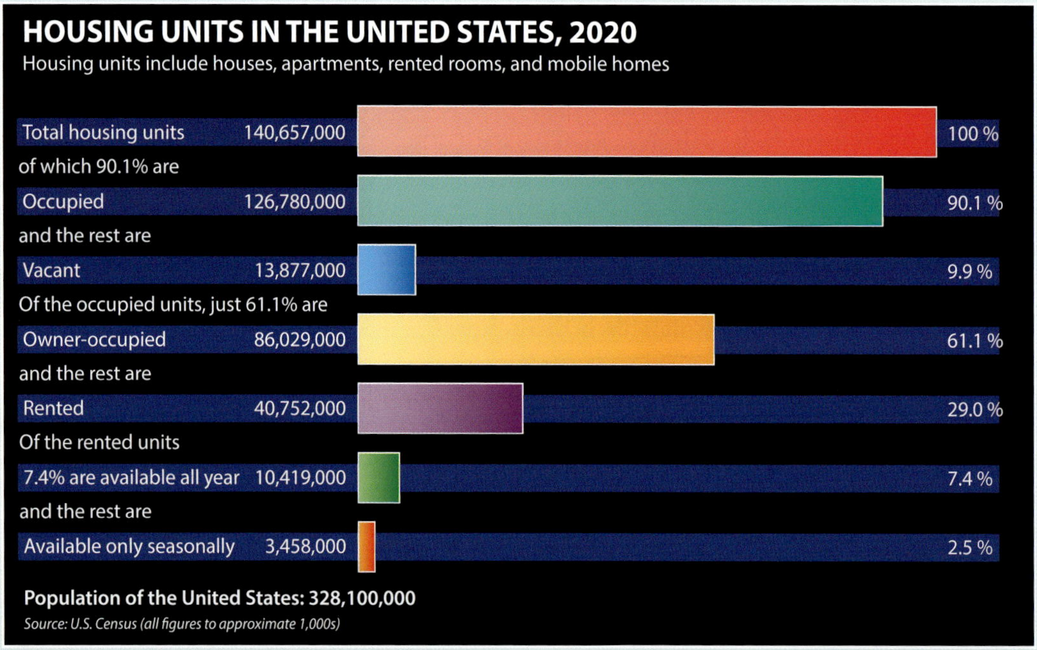

- transportation to view housing options
- asking governments to control the types of housing that property developers build.

In Vancouver, Canada, Housing Action for Local Taxpayers (HALT) has made the government put new taxes in place to keep house prices from spiraling out of control. It has helped, and prices are down 17 percent from their highest point. In Seattle, one in nine people live below the poverty line and homelessness is growing. There, activists such as Architects for Affordable Housing point out the growing gap between luxury apartments, ordinary homes, and shelters for the homeless. Advocacy groups have pushed for taxes similar to those imposed in Vancouver.

LOW RISK HIGH RISK

WHAT'S AT STAKE?

Why are some developers and homeowners against **integrating** different types of housing in one area? What effect do the words "urban ghetto" or "slum" have on the people living there?

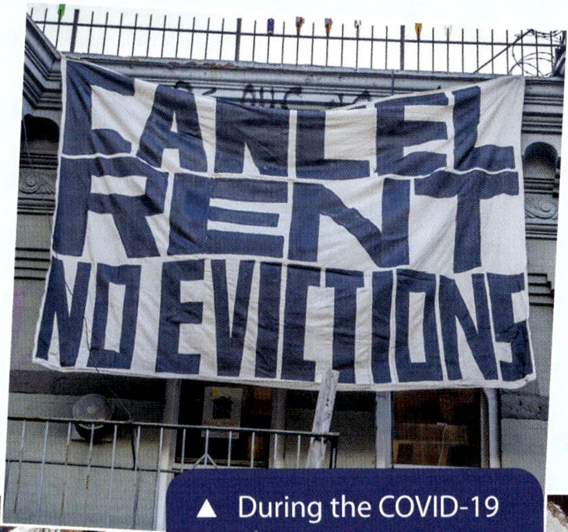

▲ During the COVID-19 pandemic, governments in the United States and Canada froze rent payments and banned **evictions**. However, these measures came to an end before the economy recovered and many tenants were still at risk of losing their housing.

◀ Public housing complexes can often have a negative reputation. Sometimes they stand out because of poor design and maintenance. Some are viewed as unsafe with higher crime rates.

WHERE IS HOMELESSNESS A PROBLEM?

Homelessness may not seem like an important issue because you don't always see the individuals that it affects. Unhoused people have to find places to eat and sleep anywhere they can, and where they won't always be forced to leave. These are often on backstreets, in parks, or out of view.

Homeless people and families sometimes stay at shelters. A shelter is a building that provides temporary residence. It gives them a secure place to rest and sleep. Many shelters also provide food or **counseling** services. Some shelters are focused on housing certain groups such as youths, women, or families. Unhoused people in addiction treatment centers often go to shelters once they have finished with the program. Shelters also provide homes for people released from a local jail or state prison.

Many homeless people have to resort to "sleeping rough." This means they spend the night in doorways, parks, under bridges, in stairwells, abandoned buildings, parking garages, or in vehicles. Unless you know to look in these places, you might not realize how many unhoused people there are in your community. Sleeping rough affects a person's physical and mental health. It also makes it difficult for them to complete housing or job applications because they have no permanent address.

▶ During the recession and economic troubles of 2008, the number of people in the United States who lost their homes because they couldn't pay their mortgages more than doubled. They had to sell most of their possessions and move to cheaper homes—if they could find them.

▼ During the COVID-19 pandemic, many people in Los Angeles, California, lost their jobs and couldn't afford the high rent in the city. Those who could lived in trailers parked on streets.

CITIES IN THE USA WITH THE MOST UNHOUSED PEOPLE

Total number of homeless in 2019 is 567,715

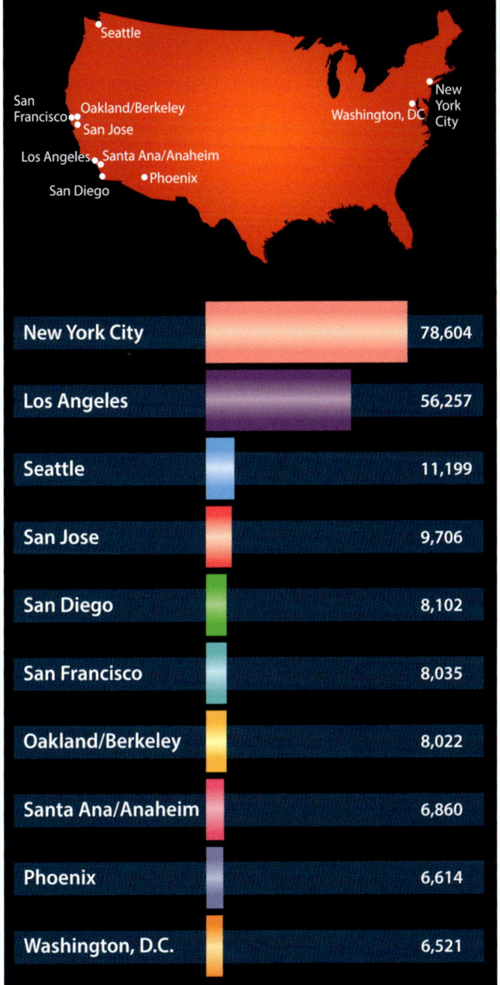

Source: U.S. Department of Housing and Urban Development

UNHOUSED YOUTHS IN USA, 2019

Youths are likely to be made homeless as a result of abuse at home.

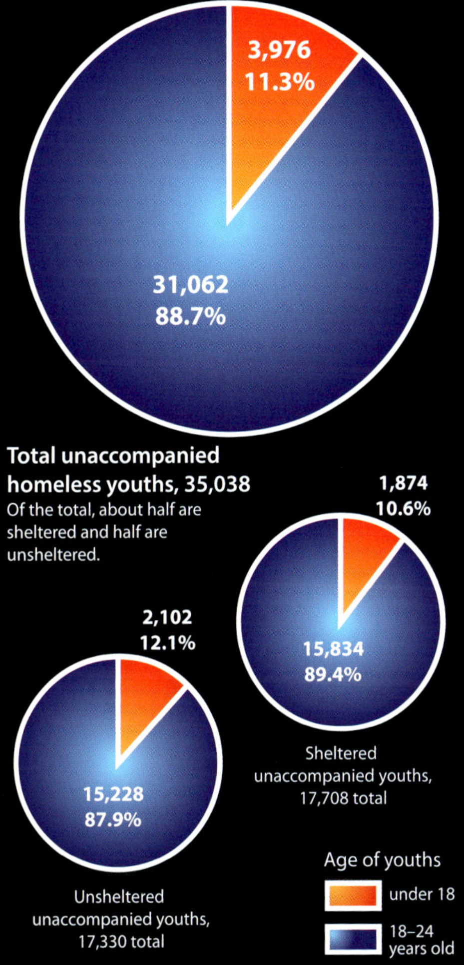

Source: U.S. Department of Housing and Urban Development

STIGMA AND SEGREGATION

Homeless people may hide their situation because of the **stigma** that goes along with homelessness. They are often judged as lazy and unwilling to work. Public housing has also been used as a way to segregate, or separate, people based on race. Historically, banks were known to discriminate against African Americans by refusing mortgages to buy homes or loans to repair homes. This form of lending descrimination was called redlining. It led to Black communities being starved of resources, lowered property values, and poorer rental options.

HOMELESS SERVICES

Ending homelessness is not as simple as providing more shelters. Issues relating to finding, affording, and holding on to safe and secure housing are very complex. The reasons why some people struggle with housing problems are as different as the individuals themselves. For example, people fleeing natural disasters or war need food, clothing, medicine, and toiletries. People escaping **domestic violence**, or unsafe family situations, benefit from counseling and housing support programs. Legal clinics, or free legal advice, are services that could help them move forward with their lives. Unhoused people struggling with mental health issues or addiction problems have another set of needs. Harm reduction programs, health clinics, and counseling could address some of the underlying causes of their housing problems.

MANY ISSUES ALL AT ONCE

People in areas dealing with war or natural disasters may become homeless overnight. Along with people facing a change in their finances because of job loss, separation, or illness, these groups may need the services of a housing help center, employment assistance, information about government programs they might qualify for, debt reduction advice, and access to computers.

◄ A soup kitchen is the term for a place where free food is served to homeless people. In the United States, it is estimated that between about 12 and 21 million people a year rely on soup kitchens.

Unhoused people dealing with several of these factors at once often find it too difficult to seek help themselves. Those sleeping rough may need street outreach workers to come to them. Drop-in centers and extra beds in shelters for extreme cold or heat can be the difference between life and death for these people.

Research shows that drop-in centers, public libraries, health clinics, ID clinics that help people register for citizenship and health services, hospitals, and food banks are the services that are used the most. Despite these services, homelessness is rising across North America. Events such as the economic downturn from the COVID-19 pandemic have made the problem worse.

WHAT'S AT STAKE?
Which groups are most affected by a crisis when it hits? How might affordable housing change the impact a crisis has on a vulnerable person?

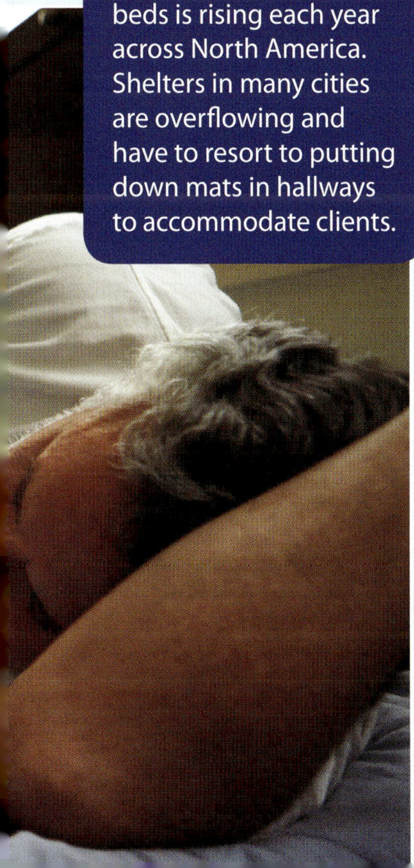

▼ The number of people needing shelter beds is rising each year across North America. Shelters in many cities are overflowing and have to resort to putting down mats in hallways to accommodate clients.

COST OF HOMELESSNESS IN CANADA, 2019

Five different ways of housing a homeless person and their comparable average costs to the authorities for a month. (Figures updated from 2016 report.)

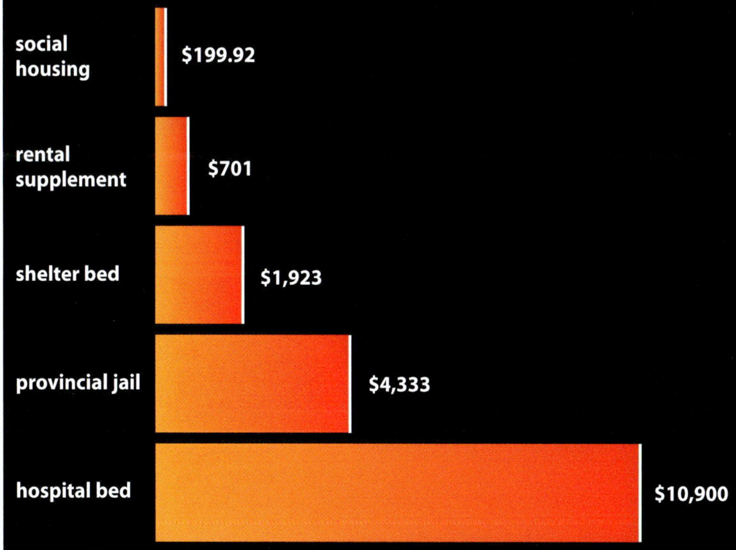

Providing supports such as social housing, rental supplements, and shelters is less expensive than the cost of a person being in jail or the hospital.

Source: Homeless Hub, Canada

FINDING A HOME

Finding affordable housing or public housing often means being on a waiting list. Wait lists are a way to match people in need with suitable housing. Wait times in the United States average about nine months but for some people, especially larger families, that can stretch to seven years.

In the United States, the National Low Income Housing Coalition reports that the federal government's Housing Choice Voucher programs close when waiting lists fill up. Some of those lists might be closed for a year at a time. Families with children make up about half of wait-list applicants. Seniors and people with disabilities also make up a large portion of those needing affordable housing. Often, unhoused people need help gathering the information to fill out these applications. If they can't complete this step, they may never succeed in finding a home.

ASK YOUR OWN QUESTIONS

Think of gaps in the ways your community helps people in a housing crisis. Brainstorm with friends for ways to fill those gaps.

▼ During the COVID-19 pandemic, an area in front of City Hall in San Francisco, California, was officially divided and marked up into socially distanced areas for homeless people to pitch their tents. Outreach vans and soup kitchens were set up to provide health checks and food for those in need.

HOUSE PRICES RISING FASTER THAN INCOMES

In the United States, in the past 50 years, average annual incomes and property rents have increased gradually. Average house prices, though, have doubled. And in cities such as San Francisco (SF) and New York, rents have soared.

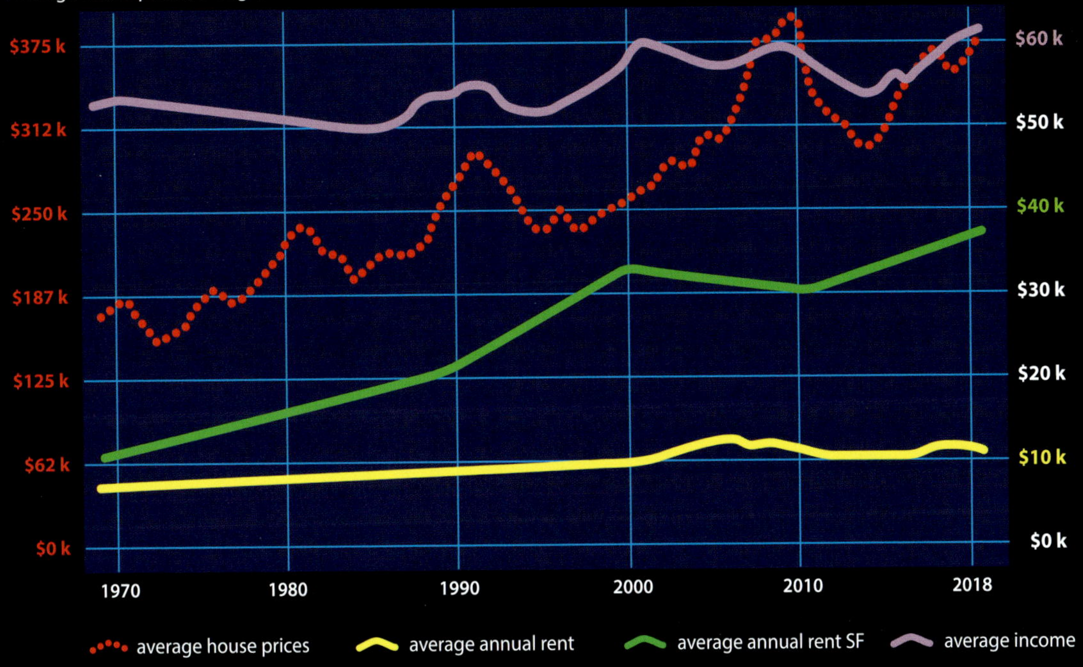

Source: U.S. Census Bureau/Stanford University/statista.com

PREFERRING TO SLEEP ROUGH

A small portion of unhoused people don't want permanent housing. There are many reasons for this, including:

- wanting to move out of areas they are currently in
- not liking social housing
- lack of trust in people offering help
- wanting money and a job first
- not wanting to discuss legal issues they have
- a feeling that applying for housing is difficult or **degrading**
- the housing waiting lists are too long
- trying to save money by being homeless
- believing they are not **eligible** for housing and don't bother to apply.

Some unhoused people will even refuse to go to shelters. They are concerned about the lack of privacy in them, theft of their possessions, bedbugs and lice, violence and abuse, and strict rules that limit their freedoms. They prefer to sleep rough.

Outreach vans are vehicles operated by charity groups to help people without shelter. They drive around looking for vulnerable people and offer many services. They will transport them to a shelter if they wish, or offer food and/or clothing, and/or blankets. They also provide information on support for mental health issues, addiction treatment centers, and counseling. Many thousands of these vans operate daily.

4 SUSPENDING JUDGMENT

Everyone has their own viewpoint, or opinion, on a topic. When you focus only on one side of a controversial issue, you can't always make the best conclusions or decisions. It is important to see how homelessness affects all parts of society and all types of people.

> *Shelter Network's programs and services are a rainbow in the clouds for homeless children and adults.*
>
> Maya Angelou, American poet and civil rights activist

◀ In June 2020, protestors in Los Angeles, California, demanded that police and the Apartment Association of Greater L.A. stop their discrimination and injustices against certain racial groups. They wanted rent cancellation, protection from landlords who harass them, and more shelters for homeless people in the downtown area.

PROVIDING THE BEST SUPPORT

When certain people are ignored, denied support, or discriminated against, they are marginalized. Marginalized groups include Indigenous peoples, people of color, immigrants, refugees, and the LGTBQ community. Black Americans make up only 13 percent of the population of the United States, but they are 40 percent of the homeless population. Veterans make up about 33 percent of unhoused males. Marginalized people are more at risk for inadequate or a lack of permanent housing. This is because of the discrimination they face in finding jobs, applying for rental units, or qualifying for support programs.

Researchers across North America have found that marginalized people with housing issues respond best to a diverse team of helpers who represent different cultures, languages, races, and lifestyles. It also helps them to have staff who have experienced homelessness themselves.

The roots and causes of homelessness are different from one individual to another. This means finding solutions based on each person's needs is more effectivc than trying to make all unhoused people fit into rigid programs and systems. The person-centered approach needs more time, money, and effort from social services, but gets the best results.

VULNERABLE GROUPS

A large number of unhoused people are dealing with mental illness or alcohol or drug addiction. Often both. These health issues are a major cause of homelessness. It is very difficult to make safe and healthy decisions for yourself and your family when your mind and body are not at their best.

People dealing with addiction and mental illness are more likely to lose their jobs, insurance, and housing. This leads to higher levels of stress, anxiety, **depression**, and substance abuse. This, of course, makes their mental illness worse and can result in addiction to even more dangerous substances.

Some areas are adopting a "Housing First" approach. This means not demanding that applicants meet certain standards before they get housing.

KEY PLAYERS

The **National Coalition for the Homeless (NCH)** is a network of helpers in the USA that includes activists, people who are or have been homeless, and advocates, all with a mission to end homelessness. It runs the **Bringing America Home Campaign**. The NCH wants to make sure that the rights and needs of unhoused people are respected and protected.

HOMELESS BY RACE AND ETHNICITY IN THE UNITED STATES

Black Americans, multiracial Americans, and Hispanics/Latinxs are far more likely to be homeless than White Americans and Asians. Pacific Islanders and Native Americans have the highest proportion of people who are homeless.

Based on figures for homeless people in the United States in 2019.

Source: National Alliance to End Homelessness, USA

▲ In 2019, city workers in Austin, Texas, watch as a woman removes her belongings from a homeless camp under a highway overpass. The camp was ordered to be cleared out. People were told to go to shelters, but the shelters were already overcrowded or completely full.

The idea is that once people who are dealing with addiction and health problems have **stable** housing, they will be better able to turn their attention to the underlying issues. After housing is arranged, then support services are offered. Part of the Housing First model is to help people reach out and become part of their local community. Being connected with other people, activities, and services makes people feel less isolated and therefore less likely to slide back into harmful behaviors.

ONE ISSUE LEADS TO ANOTHER

In the United States, statistics show that 38 percent of unhoused people are dependent on alcohol, while 26 percent depend on other harmful drugs. For many, addiction was the result of homelessness, not the other way around. The harsh conditions of living on the street, including food shortages, the effects of weather, and being separated from loved ones, sometimes makes people turn to mind-altering substances as a coping method.

As more people face the crisis of poor or no housing, homelessness becomes more visible. Public awareness about the issue increases when homeless people are viewed as humans with feelings, needs, and problems like anyone else, and not as vagrants or threats to public safety. Some business owners argue that homeless people are a threat to businesses because some customers are less likely to visit areas where homelessness is visible.

People often have a "not in my backyard" mentality when it comes to shelters or drop-in centers for homeless people. Some worry that the value of their property might go down if shelters or low-cost housing are built in their neighborhood. This stigma and discrimination pushes unhoused peopled farther away from the services and supports they need.

CHANGING ATTITUDES

When some people see homeless people walking with their possessions or sleeping rough, they may not have empathy for their situation. They don't always understand that they are often caught in difficult circumstances. A few may see homeless people as lazy, weak-willed, or a threat.

▲ In August 2020, advocates for more services for homeless people clashed with residents concerned about the number of shelters in their residential area in Toronto, Ontario, Canada. With the price of housing in the city soaring, more and more people are pushed out of the housing market each year.

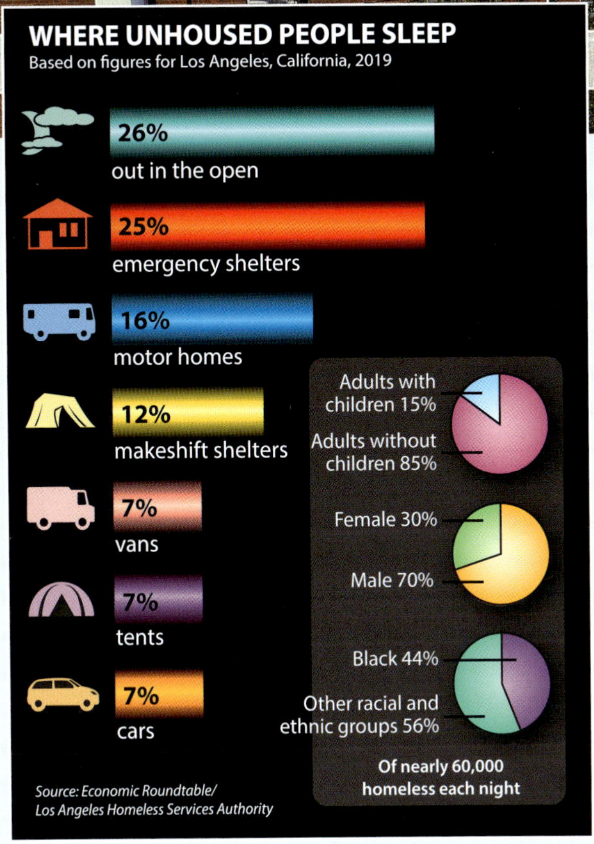

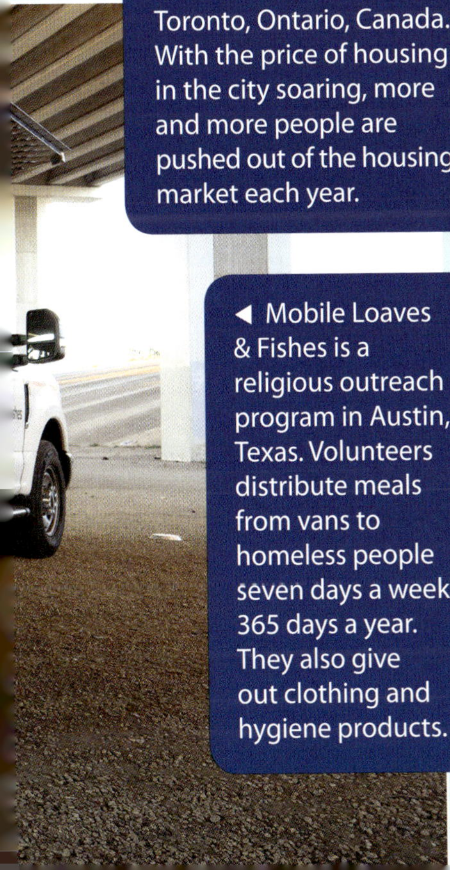

◀ Mobile Loaves & Fishes is a religious outreach program in Austin, Texas. Volunteers distribute meals from vans to homeless people seven days a week, 365 days a year. They also give out clothing and hygiene products.

A person's attitude toward homeless people affects what they think the solution to their problem should be. When homelessness is seen as a consequence of bad decisions or poor choices, the solution is often to punish them or hide them away. When people understand they could be in that same position with a sudden job loss, death in the family, or major illness, they become more **compassionate** and supportive of programs that assist. The solution then shifts to more services, support, and resources to help people live with dignity.

Studies have shown that people change their attitudes when they interact with homeless people by volunteering at shelters or by spending time talking to them on a personal level. They begin to see unhoused people as individuals, and are willing to support organizations and governments that assist and fund housing programs.

5 WHERE THINGS STAND

Across North America, cities and regions are looking at new ways of providing affordable, adequate housing for an increasing number of people. They want to do this by providing more than just two choices for housing: rental or homeownership. However, this requires a shift in attitude of all the key players in housing and urban planning.

> *"Safe, adequate, and affordable housing is essential to building strong families, strong communities, and a strong economy."*
>
> Justin Trudeau, Prime Minister of Canada

KEY PLAYERS

Investment in Affordable Housing (IAH) in Canada provides federal funding for affordable housing through the Canada Mortgage and Housing Corporation (CMHC). Funds are used for new construction, renovations, homeownership assistance, and contributions toward rent payments. Since 2011, more than 400,000 households have received funding from the IAH.

◀ San Jose, California, is one of the hardest places in the United States to buy a home. "Measure E" is a tax on the sale of San Jose properties worth $2 million or more. It has helped slow the construction of more expensive homes and encourages homebuilders to build affordable homes, like this multifamily complex.

NEW TYPES OF HOME OWNERSHIP

Cities supporting new affordable housing plans often need to update their land development bylaws to balance urban sprawl and restore **inner city** areas. When bylaws ensure that newly built neighborhoods include housing geared to a mix of income levels, it helps lessen precarious housing and make neighborhoods more stable.

Some new affordable housing ideas include:

- **Build-to-rent**: This is more than just a group of rental houses. It is a complex of rental homes with facilities such as a swimming pool, and tennis courts. They are usually managed by a private company.
- **Housing cooperatives:** People who live in co-ops are members and not tennants. They are non-profit, so the rent increases are voted on and usually go up to cover costs, including such things as new roofs. Basic maintenance such as grass cutting, is often shared. Some units have rent that is based on low income so people can live affordably there long-term.
- **Shared ownership**: This gives first-time home buyers a chance to own a share in a building. The purchasers pay a mortgage on the share they own, and pay rent to a housing association for the remaining share. Purchasers can increase their share over time up to full ownership.
- **Community land trust**: This is a corporation that holds land on behalf of a community. It looks after the buildings, parks, and businesses in an area. It keeps prices affordable and stable so low and moderate income residents can have good housing at fair prices.

The goal of ending homelessness is difficult, but not impossible. The solution needs to include many different strategies to address all the factors and causes that lead to precarious housing and homelessness. One of the first things most experts agree on is that there needs to be a community-wide approach. It is important for facilities, services, and housing programs to coordinate their work so it is efficient and clients can access all eligible support. When organizations overlap, or all types of services are not offered in one area, homeless and precariously housed people can fall between the cracks. This is especially true for the most vulnerable such as people with serious health problems, people at risk of violence, and people who belong to marginalized groups that are traditionally overlooked or denied access to good, affordable housing.

Another vital part of ending homelessness is rapid re-housing. People who find themselves without a suitable home or any home at all should not spend months and years waiting for somewhere to live. The longer a person has unstable housing, the worse their health conditions tend to become.

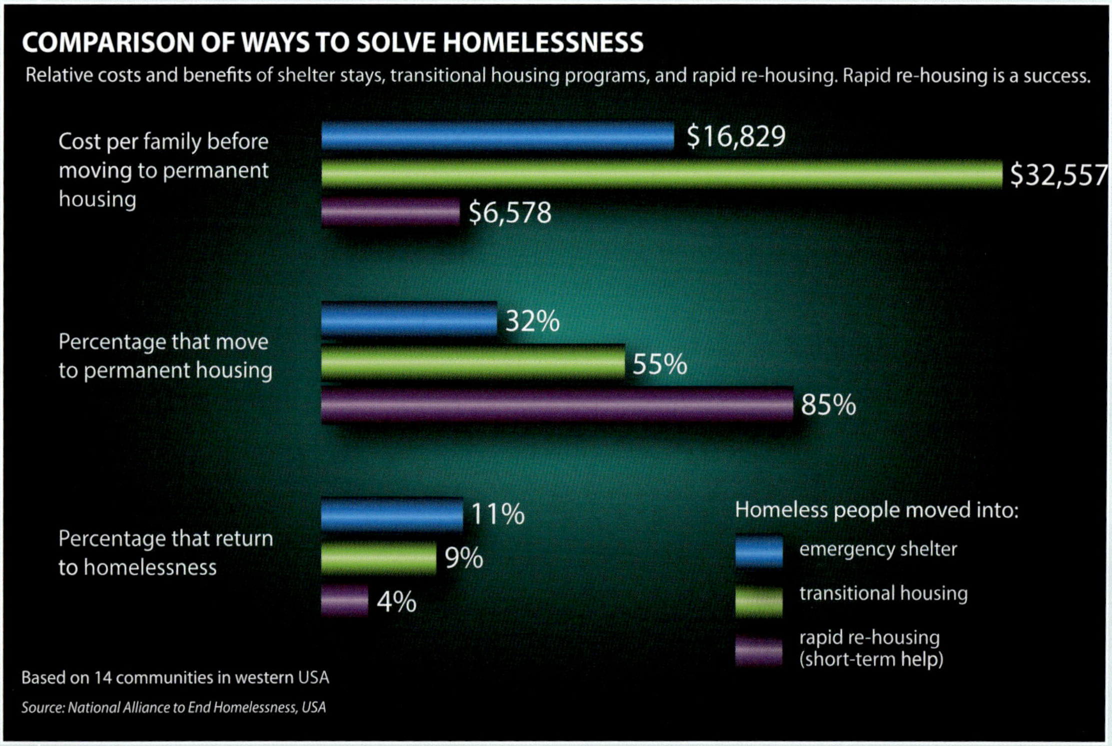

▲ Protest buttons have been popular since the early 1900s. Buttons or pins with slogans are a way for people to support a cause and draw attention to social issues.

▲ Building "tiny houses," like these in Detroit, Michigan, for homeless people is a growing trend. These are often considered temporary homes, while social services find permanent homes.

LESSONS FROM ABROAD

For rapid re-housing, communities need a crisis response plan. This is a step-by-step strategy for handling emergency housing situations. Someone leaving an abusive or violent situation will need help quickly and without much advance warning. A long-term solution to prevent homelessness includes improving job opportunities, rehabilitation programs, and a basic income for everyone.

Some critics believe we will never be able to end homelessness. But some countries have been successful in tackling the problem. In Finland, the number of unhoused people has gone down in recent years. It has almost eliminated absolute homelessness, or those sleeping rough, and has found ways to assist precariously housed people. Housing groups have done this by converting shelters to permanent low-cost housing, often with counseling services on site.

ASK YOUR OWN QUESTIONS

If you had a conversation with your local government representative, what would you ask them about the housing plan for your area?

When a topic is discussed often and by many people, some information can be misunderstood or misheard. Sometimes people believe something so strongly, they present their opinion as fact. This can lead to the creation of myths, which are widely held but false beliefs or ideas.

The following are myths about homelessness that prevent people from finding compassion for unhoused people and from focusing on helping them find a way out of their situation.

- ***Being homeless is a choice***

Anyone can make a mistake, but homeless people are often the victims of unexpected and unwanted events. A serious illness can ruin a family financially if they do not have health coverage. A sudden job loss can make debts soar. Violence or abuse can force people to escape to a safer environment. No one leaves their home to be cold, hungry, and unsafe unless they feel they have no other choice.

ASK YOUR OWN QUESTIONS

What questions can you ask yourself to figure out if something is a myth or fact? Are you more likely to read or hear myths on social media, news sites, or government reports? Why?

▼ Charities such as the Bread of Life mission in Seattle, Washington, provide support for people of all levels of housing. This includes homeowners and the employed who do not have income left over for food, services, and insurance after struggling to pay rent.

▲ In 2020, Helen Rosenthal was one of the New York City councilors to write to the city mayor to ask that the homeless living in hotels should not be moved to other locations during the COVID-19 pandemic.

- ***All homeless people are alcoholics or addicts***

According to the Substance Abuse and Mental Health Services Administration (SAMHSA), about one third of unhoused people have substance abuse problems. However, studies have found that drug addiction and alcoholism are often a result of being homeless and not always the reason an individual becomes homeless.

- ***Homeless people are lazy and just don't want to work***

An Urban Institute survey in the United States found that about 44 percent of homeless people had paid work. Some work full time. But this does not mean they can afford housing. Studies in Canada and the United States found that workers who earn minimum wage could not afford a one- or two-bedroom apartment at Fair Market Rent anywhere.

- ***Homelessness will never happen to me***

Losing permanent housing can happen to anyone. A set of unfortunate and unexpected events can result in a housing crisis. As the gap between the wealthiest and poorest levels of society widens and the economy struggles, more people will become vulnerable to losing a safe and affordable place to live.

GLOBAL DISASTERS AND PANDEMICS

Homelessness usually affects a few people at a time, but some events can cause thousands of people to have a housing crisis all at once. This puts incredible pressure on housing services.

Natural disasters such as tornadoes, monsoons, forest fires, and earthquakes can destroy buildings and other structures in just hours, leading to a sudden need for emergency housing. Most times, areas are not equipped to handle these situations, even if they are prepared. In 2017, Hurricane Harvey hit Texas and Louisiana. The winds, heavy rains, and flooding caused major damage. More than 135,000 homes were damaged or destroyed. Three years after the storm, some people still hadn't been able to repair their homes.

DEALING WITH THE AFTERMATH

Human-made disasters can be self-inflicted—such as wars and terrorist attacks—or accidental, such as the explosion in August 2020 in Beirut, Lebanon. A warehouse near the docks in the city contained fertilizer that exploded. In an instant, the blast killed 220 people and left about 300,000 homeless. Emergency shelters had to house more than 1,000 extra people the night of the explosion, and 10,000 after that. Many people continue to live in houses so badly damaged they could collapse at any time, but they have nowhere else to go.

During the global COVID-19 pandemic in 2020, with economies shut down and many living in lockdown, unemployment skyrocketed. People had no income. In countries where the government did not step in to provide financial relief, people faced being evicted from rental units or **defaulting** on their mortgages. Some countries set up programs to provide basic incomes to people and keep them housed.

KEY PLAYERS

The **National Alliance to End Homelessness (NAEH)** in the United States and the **Canadian Alliance to End Homelessness (CAEH)** lead national groups of individuals, organizations, and communities. They are working together to end homelessness in North America. Both groups believe all people have a right to safe, decent, permanent, and affordable housing. They focus on putting those beliefs into everyday action.

▶ From August to October 2020, fires raged across northern California. More than 10,000 structures burned—among them this house in Juniper Hills.

▶ Foreclosure is the legal process in which a bank takes back a property that the owner has stopped making payments for. The property is then sold, sometimes at an auction, for the bank to get back its money. The COVID-19 pandemic and job losses forced many people into foreclosure on their homes.

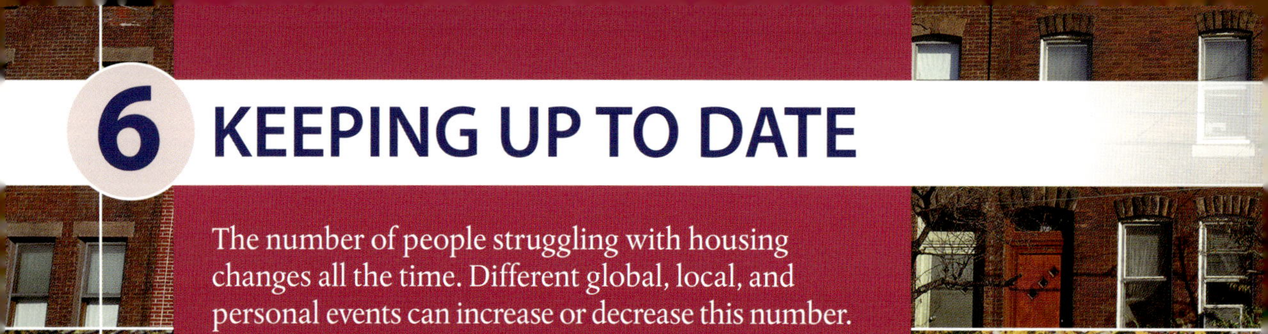

6 KEEPING UP TO DATE

The number of people struggling with housing changes all the time. Different global, local, and personal events can increase or decrease this number. Homelessness is a social issue with many underlying factors. Some address it as a human rights issue. Others as a personal issue. You need to constantly monitor the situation to be able to react and, if necessary, to change your views and actions on housing and homelessness.

ASK YOUR OWN QUESTIONS

What is your own bias on the issues of housing and homelessness? How might it affect which news sources you research? How can you balance your **news diet** to make up for your personal bias? What can you do to help?

SEARCH TIPS

When looking at websites, address extensions can help pinpoint what sort of information you may be getting:

.gov (government)—restricted to use by government entities.

.org (organization)—anyone can register for this, although it is often used for nonprofit organizations and charities.

.com (commercial)—originally for businesses, it is the most widely used extension.

Country extensions:
.ca Canada
.au Australia
.uk United Kingdom
.ru Russia
.de Germany

◀ The world's biggest refugee camp is the Kutupalong camp in Bangladesh. Rohingya people were forced to flee the neighboring country of Myanmar because of their race and religion. Now, more than 850,000 people in the camp are looking for a permanent home.

SPREAD YOUR RESEARCH NET WIDE

Why is it important to keep up to date on what is happening with affordable housing and homelessness? One reason is that homelessness often goes hand in hand with other problems such as natural disasters and addiction. By dealing with the lack of housing for individuals and families in need, those problems are also being addressed. Another reason is that the housing issue is a problem that society can solve.

Many people have come up with creative ideas to help end homelessness and the shortage of affordable housing. This includes building small home communities or **repurposing** buildings to become affordable properties. Homelessness can be decreased if we offer help instead of ignoring the problem. Understanding the causes and factors that lead to homelessness reminds us that circumstances can change for everyone and put anyone at risk. This affects society as a whole.

So how can you keep up to date? Remember that not all information is broadcast to the public. Sometimes you have to seek it out yourself. The Internet is a good place to start. Search engines will point you to all types of organizations, committees, and charities that are already working on the problem. Some of these are international such as the Institute of Global Homelessness. Others are local and service your area, such as church and Nextdoor groups. Learning about these levels of support for unhoused people gives you a more balanced view of what is being done and how you can contribute to solving the crisis.

AUDIT YOUR NEWS DIET

Getting informed and keeping informed on a topic relies on finding reliable sources and accurate information. Auditing your news diet means checking what information you are getting and where it is coming from. You should do an audit every few months to make sure false or misleading information hasn't crept into your source material. First, verify who is creating your source material. Are they an expert on the subject, or have they included experts' data? Check the **agenda** of the organizations you might follow to make sure it isn't slanting the focus of their reports. Make note of the bias your sources might have so you can determine what and how information is presented.

MAKE SURE YOU HAVE A BALANCED VIEW

For housing and homelessness, source material could include government statistics, homelessness advocates, community outreach programs, international programs, local **initiatives**, and personal interviews. To check the credibility of sources, refer to the Ask Your Own Questions box on page 12.

To keep up to date on the topic on the Internet, use news aggregator sites that collect relevant articles, data, and websites, such as The Homeless Hub. You can also set up Google alerts for a related word or phrase.

When you feel you have a good understanding of homelessness and housing problems, you might want to get involved to make a positive change. You can start at the local level and work to make a difference in your own neighborhood, community, or city. You can also look at ways you can help on a bigger scale. Encouraging governments at all levels to change laws to clear the way for more affordable housing, and providing services for unhoused people, can bring changes. The more voices that join together to raise awareness and make a difference, the fewer people there will be that face a housing crisis in their lives.

SEARCH TIPS

When searching for a topic, such as homelessness, online:

- Use quotation marks around a phrase to search for that exact combination of words (for example, "sleeping rough").
- Use a colon and an extension to search a specific site (for example, Addiction: gov for all government website mentions of the topic).
- Use the word Define and a colon to search for word definitions (for example, Define: foreclosure).

◀ Different media formats make it easier to get informed and stay informed. Information is made available anywhere at any time.

GLOSSARY

activist A person who campaigns to bring about changes

adequate Meets a specific need

agenda An underlying or hidden plan of action

clickbait An online encouragement to read or hear something

compassionate Feeling concern for others

complexes Built-up areas with many similar living spaces and services

cooperatives Buildings owned and run by its members

counseling Professional help and advice

credible Trustworthy and believable

defaulting Not able to repay a loan or mortgage

degrading Shameful

denser More closely packed together

depression A mental illness that causes sadness and loss of interest in daily life

dignity Sense of pride in oneself

direct action Doing something that gets an immediate result

discrimination Act of treating someone with less favor than other people

domestic violence Abusive and aggressive behavior in the home from one family member toward another

economy The business, finances, and resources of an area

eligible Satisfying the conditions to do something

empathy The ability to understand the feelings of others

evictions Getting people to move out of homes for not paying rent or for breaking rules

Great Depression The economic crisis that began in 1929 and ended during WWII

hindered Delayed or blocked

Indigenous The first inhabitants of a place

initiatives New plans

inner city The center of a city, with older and poorer housing stock

integrating Mixing in to make whole or as one

mass immigration Large numbers of people from other countries entering a country to live and work

minimum wage The lowest wage allowed by law; it is not necessarily enough to pay all living costs

news diet The information you take in each day

objective Not taking one side over another

oral Spoken

petition Write a request, usually signed by many people, to get something changed

population density The number of people living in a unit of area

recession An economic situation in which trade and industrial activity slow down

refugees People coming into a country to live after fleeing their country because of war or natural disaster

repurposing Finding a new use for

shantytowns Areas of small, poorly built houses, usually on the edges of towns

stable Not likely to change

statistics Data presented as numbers and figures

stigma A label of disgrace and shame

subsidizing Being helped with the cost from an outside group

systemic racism Discrimination that is so widespread, it is found in all parts of society

treaties Binding agreements between governments and Indigenous peoples

visual An image that provides information

vulnerable At risk

SOURCE NOTES

QUOTATIONS

Page 4: www.nytimes.com/2020/01/22/us/california-homeless-people-stories.html

Page 9: Stegner, Wallace. *Angle of Repose.* Vintage, 2014.

Page 14: www.doonething.org/quotes/homeless-quotes.htm

Page 27: www.doonething.org/quotes/homeless-quotes.htm

Page 32: www.homelesshub.ca/toolkit/liberal-party-canada-platform-0

REFERENCES USED FOR THIS BOOK

Chapter 1: The Housing Situation, pages 4–7

https://bit.ly/3nywCQ2
https://bit.ly/2MT3KWf
https://bit.ly/39ga3e8
https://bit.ly/35uwWJz

Chapter 2: How to Get Informed, pages 8–13

https://bit.ly/3s7A341
https://bit.ly/39kBvqR
https://bit.ly/35oJNgk
https://bit.ly/3i1a8pO
https://bit.ly/3bDMnmP

Chapter 3: Homelessness Issues, pages 14–25

https://bit.ly/3i26fkz
https://www.habitat.org
https://bit.ly/39jifKv
https://bit.ly/3qdrYch
https://bit.ly/39k72t5
https://bit.ly/3bz1xJE

Chapter 4: Suspending Judgment, pages 26–31

https://bit.ly/3bqupDT
https://mlf.org
https://bit.ly/38vACwq
https://www.dav.org
https://bit.ly/39jil4P

Chapter 5: Where Things Stand, pages 32–39

https://bit.ly/2Xu5pDC
https://bit.ly/3bufJUm
https://bit.ly/35nJ2nR
https://bit.ly/38whoHf
https://bit.ly/2LE37z0

Chapter 6: Keeping Up to Date, pages 40–43

https://ighomelessness.org
https://bit.ly/3q8LS8c
https://bit.ly/3sbAcTL
https://nyti.ms/2LbOxPL
https://ab.co/35uxz5T

FIND OUT MORE

Finding good source material on the Internet can sometimes be a challenge. When analyzing how reliable the information is, consider these points:

- Who is the author of the page? Is it an expert in the field or a person who experienced the event?
- Is the site well known and up to date? A page that has not been updated for several years probably has out-of-date information.
- Can you verify the facts with another site? Always double-check information.
- Have you checked all possible sites? Don't just look on the first page a search engine provides.
- Remember to try government sites and research papers.
- Have you recorded website addresses and names? Keep this data so you can backtrack later and verify the information you want to use.

WEBSITES

Read the stories of teenage homeless youth in their own words:
https://bit.ly/3hYAKb7

Check out nine ways you can help homeless people:
www.lascandal.org/9-ways-can-help-homeless

Watch this PBS video about how a community came together to help students struggling with homelessness:
https://to.pbs.org/39iTHRU

Learn about an organization that helps people around the world build or improve a place they can call home:
www.habitat.org/ap

Research an organization that helps homeless children and youths:
www.covenanthouse.org

BOOKS

Applegate, Katherine. *Crenshaw*. Feiwel and Friends, 2017.

Jacobson, Jennifer Richard. *The Dollar Kids*. Candlewick, 2020.

Jamieson, Victoria, and Omar Mohamed. *When Stars Are Scattered*. Dial Books for Young Readers, 2020.

Ogle, Rex. *Free Lunch*. Norton Young Readers, 2019.

Rhodes, Jewell Parker. *Towers Falling*. Little, Brown & Company, 2016.

Svetcov, Danielle. *Parked*. Dial Books for Young Readers, 2020.

Venkatraman, Padma. *The Bridge Home*. Nancy Paulsen Books, 2019.

Yang, Kelly. *Front Desk*. Arthur A. Levine Books/Scholastic Inc., 2018.

ABOUT THE AUTHOR

Natalie Hyde has written more than 80 books, both fiction and nonfiction, for young readers. When not writing, she enjoys researching her family tree and feeding her chickens.

INDEX